FERN OUR BABY DEER

True Friends!

Linda Sund

Dedication

For further information, write to MAC THE RAVEN ENTERPRISES, LLC

P.O. BOX 1186

Hoodsport, WA 98548

mactheraven@gmail.com

Order online at www.mactheraven.com

Library of Congress Control Number

International Standard Book Number: 978-0-9893597-7-1

Mac Meets Fern

Our Pet Raven - A True Story

Written By: Linda Sund

Illustrated by: Denis Proulx

Book 4 of a Series

Sharing stories of Mac's Adventures.

Coming soon: "Mac Meets Leeanne", "Mac's First Day At School",

"Mac Hikes Mt. Ellinor"

With love and special thanks to my step-daughter Julie Sund Nichols. She took time from her busy schedule and edited my books. Julie added a special flair to the words that only a mother could do.

Especially for: Rylee, Kale, Sarah, and Trevor

Love, Nana & Papa

Order on-line   www.mactheraven.com

Today,
Mac woke up
to a loud noise.
It's Papa Brian, and he's out
standing by the family van.
There is something inside!

Mama Linda runs over and says,
"Oh My!
You have a baby deer
lying there on her side.
She's hurt!
Let's get rid of the dirt
and take a look at her eyes."
Linda lets out a big sigh.

Mac rushes over
because he wants to see.
Mac wonders:
What have we here?
... as he sits by her knee.

It's a fawn!

Brian lays her down on the lawn.

She is only about one week old,

and this little one is really cold.

Papa Brian rescued this little deer.

What in the world happened here???

Linda comes right back,
this time with a black sack.
She pulls out a warm blanket,
then Mac's old turkey baster!
This time it's filled with goat's milk.
The baby deer is thirsty,
and though she is small,
her fur shines like silk.
She is brown all over
with white dots - -
lots, and lots, and lots of spots.

Mac sits near,
watching that little deer.
He keeps eyeing those spots.
Mac tries and tries to pick them out,
and gets frustrated when he cannot!
AWK! AWK! AWK!
Mac thinks:
I've never seen spots like these!
Someone help me get them out,
please, please!

Mama Linda
walks over and says,
"Mac, stop that and be nice.
You know better than that.
Don't be naughty
like that big old cat."

As the days go on,
the fawn gets strong.
Her name is Fern
and she fits right in,
getting along.

Fern was hit by a car that turned,
and for a long while
she laid on the road.
Minutes went by,
but no cars slowed.
Finally, Papa Brian saw her
and stopped.
He gently put her in the car,
and told her she would be fine;
home wasn't far.

Fern was lucky that day,
and she is really the CUTEST,
By far!
(Do you think MAC would disagree?)

Mac learns he has
to share his space;
that will always be the case.
Ruby the dog, Clinger the cat,
and now Fern the deer...
Mac really has the best
of friends here!

The sun goes down
and there is no frown in sight.
Only happy faces here--
a campfire tonight!

We are so thankful our family grew.
Check it out! We're a happy crew!
So for now, it is time for us to say,
goodnight to you...

Mac at 2 1/2 months old sitting with Auntie Mary Ann

COMING SOON!

MAC

MEETS

LEEANNE

CPSIA information can be obtained
at www.ICGtesting.com
Printed in the USA
BVIC00n0858291114
376446BV00001B/3